ELEMENTS OF A MOTHER'S LOVE

Story by Louise Guppy-Stokely

Illustrated by Veronika Hipolito

From
Chuck S.

Elements of a Mother's Love
Copyright © 2023 by Louise Guppy-Stokely

tellwell

Tellwell Talent
www.tellwell.ca

ISBN
978-0-2288-9337-0 (Hardcover)
978-0-2288-9333-2 (Paperback)

INTRODUCTION TO ELEMENTS OF A MOTHER'S LOVE

Motherhood is to nourish, to protect, to guide, to be strong and to love her children with all her being.

While separated from her children at a great distance, how does a mother achieve this through daily life?

Mother Nature is a great healer, giving life and comfort in the many elements that our Mother Earth provides.

In the spirit of motherhood, this story was created.

To Rylie & Alex

Congratulations on your Baby Girl Aspen ~

Louise Heappy~Stokely

DEDICATION

I have had the blessing of having three mothers in my life.

My mom Catharyn, who gave me life, loved and cared for her three children very deeply beyond measure.

My mom Airdrie, my stepmother, has been a role model and guide in my life's journey from a young teen to the present.

My auntie Carolyn, my mother's identical twin, I have had a very special bond with throughout my life. This bond became more so when my mom passed away at the young age of 50.

To my daughters: Emily, Olivia, Vanessa, Kelsie and Shauna, who have grown into strong amazing women. I cherish and love them deeply.

ELEMENTS OF A MOTHER'S LOVE

I am the sun, said the mother to her children.

I will light upon you as you rise and start your day of adventure.

I will warm your rosy cheeks as you play in fallen snow. ~~

I will nourish you with nature's abundant harvest to give you health. ~~

Your tender young soul, luminous, glows with strength and vitality.

I will give you tranquility as I set in the quiet evening sky, ~~

telling you a story of soft colours that span the horizon...

I am the wind, said the mother to her children.

I will carry fallen leaves, swirling and tossing them about. You jump,

rolling in play, grasping one of our Creator's exquisite colours of nature ~~

to feel it crumple in your tiny hands.

You are a smiling ray of sunshine; your laughter echoes.

I embrace it in my heart.

I will blow a gentle breeze as you fly your kite high into the heavens. ~~

This gentle breeze will soothe you as it blows around you, ~~ lingering.

When you pick a soft fuzzy dandelion, blowing with all your might,

the delicate seeds are carried off ~~ set in flight, just as I blow you a kiss...

I am the clouds, said the mother to her children.

I will make beautiful shapes for you to enjoy. ~~

As you look up into the sky, clouds will move and change shape.

Your imagination can create wonderful stories and take you to

places far away. White and fluffy, soft and cuddly they are,

just as my hugs are to you and yours to me...

I am the rain, said the mother to her children.

I will make puddles for you to step into, jump over and splash about in.

I will refresh you as you walk along a forest path or in a park. ~~

You wonder if a rainbow will appear...

When the rain is stormy, I see your little face in the window.

You stare out, a quiet moment shared to cuddle in; warmth radiates.

Raindrops on the window glass are like crystals;

they frame your angelic face, peering out with wonder in your eyes.

I am the moon, said the mother to her children.

I will light your way in dark moments. ~~

I am here as you look up with questions about the universe.

I will answer you honestly.

Even though there will be times when I am far away, ~~

I will be as close as a prayer is to your lips.

I will be as close as your heart is to your soul.

In spirit and love, ~~ I am with you.

I am a blanket of stars in the night sky,

said the mother to her children.

I embrace you, I will protect you, I will give you hope,

I will encourage you to seek your dreams.

I will pray for guidance that angels fly close by

to light upon your shoulder and whisper words of comfort

when you may feel frightened.

I am here as you play, as you sleep, as you dream...

I am the quiet dawn, said the mother to her children.

As you wake on this day, I will warm you with good thoughts.

I will encourage you to learn and to be brave.

As the dawn and new morning brighten your world,

you brighten mine in so many ways...

Take flight, my little ones.

Seek, ~~ Live, ~~ Love.

May you have peace and my love with you always on your life's journey,

for you are a part of me ~~ as I am a part of you.

Like time, as it travels along the never-ending expanse of our universe,

I will be with you always, said the mother to her children.

ACKNOWLEDGEMENTS

To put my words out there for the world to read is a very daunting task. These words became a children's story that I have held very dear and close for 25 years.

Finding Tellwell Publishing was a blessing from my first point of contact and those that followed.

To Scott Lunn, my consultant, I thank Scott for his professional and caring nature that put my nervousness at ease. Scott was patient with my questions about publishing, taking time to understand my children's story book and why it was written.

Scott being down to earth, I felt we were on the "same page", when we had conversations.

I am grateful to you Scott and I thank you!

I was then introduced to Shaira Villamor, my project manager.

Shaira was very kind and patient also with my questions upon questions, always taking the time to answer and to make sure I was comfortable with the ongoing process of self publishing. Shaira gave me the confidence to forge ahead into the publishing world for the first time.

I trusted Shaira wholly with her wisdom and her expertise as she supported my book along this incredible journey.

I am grateful to you Shaira and I thank you!

To Veronika Hipolito my illustrator whose talent knows no bounds. With each and every draft I was so enchanted with the softness, eloquence and beauty of her work. I was brought to tears on many occasions as I approved each illustration that she created!

Veronika brought my words to life with the characters and every small nuance that she added with each illustration.

I am so grateful that I chose you to illustrate my children's story book.

I thank you Veronika!

To Jen MacBride, my editor who patiently went through my written words with a fine-toothed comb to make sure it read in the gentle beautiful flow that I intended.

I am grateful to you Jen and I thank you!

To Benjam Mosquera and GB Faelnar, the interior file work that you both did is amazing.

I thank you for your time and dedication on my book! I am grateful to both of you Benjam and GB!

To the Tellwell Publishing House, I am grateful for the existence of this company. It was so important for me to find a Canadian company, my experience has been awesome!

Printed in the USA
CPSIA information can be obtained
at www.ICGtesting.com
JSHW041803010324
58124JS00004B/12